# Manifest Your Dreams

## A Vision Board Creation Tutorial with Clip Art to Help You Achieve Your Highest Goals

### Regina Osante

# STEP # 1

## YOUR *Free*

## DOWLOADABLE BONUSES

**Your step-by-step guide to success in Wealth creation**

**Vision board Workbook for KIDS**

**Manifesting your best life Planner**

# Go to the LAST PAGE for your download instructions

Help us keep creating quality books by leaving an **honest review.**
**Your feedback means the world to us**

Find all our publications **online**

FREDDOPUB.COM/DISCOVER

or scan the **QR** code with your phone camera

# WELCOME!

This book is designed to **empower you on your journey towards realizing your dreams and aspirations.** Whether you're aiming for personal growth, career milestones, or cultivating a fulfilling life, this book will serve as your creative compass.

Inside, you'll find the step by step, exercises, prompts, and space to articulate and visualize your goals. Through the strategic curation of hundreds of images, phrases, and affirmations from the clip art book, you'll craft a **powerful and effective** vision board that resonates deeply with your highest dreams.

Beyond the creative process of assembling your Vision Board, I've incorporated an additional dimension to support your path to success: **the power of essential oils.** You'll discover essential oils that serve as catalysts for concentration, inspiration, intuition, and receptiveness to new possibilities. These aromatic companions offer more than just delicious scents — they can anchor your intentions and amplify your creative energy as you dive into the process of creating your Vision Board.

 With love, Regina

# How to navigate this book

**1** Step-by-step guide

**2** Images

| | | |
|---|---|---|
| Goals | Sports -Fitness | Checks |
| Habits | Sports | Time freedom |
| Self-care, Wellness | Hobbies | Emotions |
| Self-development, | Books writing | Travel & Places |
| Nutrition | Toys & Tools | Nature |
| Marriage | Designing & art | Countries & flags |
| Family | Home | Experiences |
| Pregnancy | Style & Fashion | Festivities |
| Babies | Business | Love & romance |
| Kids | Entrepreneurship | Friendship |
| Activities | Money | Pets |
| | | Alphabets |

**3** Quotes

| | | |
|---|---|---|
| Empowering beliefs | Mindset | Spiritual |
| Health and Wellness | Travel | Money & Abundance |

**4** Bonus Downloads

# IN THESE PAGES YOU'LL FIND

What is a vision board and why make one?

Tips to make your vision board powerful and effective

Materials needed

Tapping into the uplifting potential of essential oils as your allies on this transformative path

Emotional significance of 6 powerful essential oils

Soul reflection session

Step by step to make your board

"New Beginnings" essential oil blend recipe

Beautiful images, quotes, affirmations and abundance checks to make your board

# WHAT IS A VISION BOARD AND WHY MAKE ONE?

It is one of the most powerful visualization tools we have at our disposal. It's a daily nudge that keeps you on track toward where you want to be. It's a snapshot of your future—**the place where your dreams and goals come together to paint a picture of your ideal life.**

**It's the tangible space where your vision takes shape,** serving as a daily reminder to not give up and to actively pursue your goals.

Your Vision Board you make with the help of this book, will serve you as a visual roadmap, **igniting motivation and clarity** by aligning your aspirations, fostering focus, and propelling you towards a more purposeful and fulfilling life.

Keep in mind: "**Vision without action is merely a dream. Action without vision just passes the time. Vision with action can change the world.**"

Joel Barker

# CONSIDER THESE TIPS

- To represent wealth, use bright colors.

- Choose images of incoming wealth, not outgoing money.

- Take time to get as clear as you can on your vision; reflect on your goals (Soul Reflection session).

- Make sure it genuinely resonates with your desires and motivates you toward manifesting your dreams.

- Show yourself doing work you love and being happy, successful, inspiring others.

- Don't censor your dreams! Be certain that **ALL** is possible.

# TAKE NOTE OF THIS

**Clarity and specificity:** Be specific about what you want to achieve. Choose images, phrases, and words that represent your aspirations, ensuring clarity in your intentions.

**Genuine connection:** Select visuals and affirmations that genuinely resonate with you. Your board should evoke strong emotions and align with your values and desires!

**Visual appeal:** Arrange your Vision Board so it is aesthetically pleasing. Use images and colors that inspire you and evoke positive feelings.

**Regular review:** Place it in a visible location where you'll see it often. Schedule regular review sessions to review your goals and reinforce your intentions.

# TAKE NOTE OF THIS

**Visualization and emotions:** Spend time visualizing yourself already achieving your goals. Engage your emotions and feel the excitement and gratitude as if your dreams have already come true.

**Adapt and evolve:** Update your Vision Board as your goals evolve or change. Allow it to grow and reflect your shifting aspirations.

**Action and accountability:** Use your vision board as a guide for action. Take steps towards your goals and hold yourself accountable for the progress you make. Celebrate achievements along the way!

# STEP 1: GATHER YOUR MATERIALS

- Cardboard or thick cardstock
- This workbook with the step-by-step process, images, words, affirmations and abundance checks curated for you
- Scissors or X-acto / utility knife
- Glue
- Glitter / stamps / stickers / craft items to use for decorating
- Photo of yourself that you **LOVE**, where you are joyous and happy

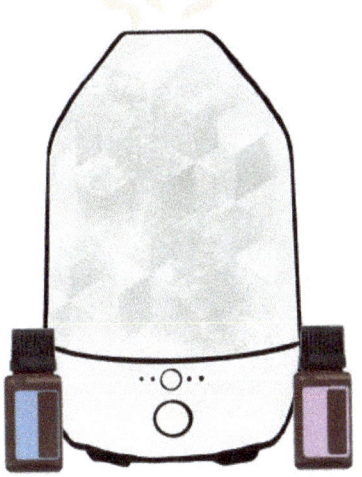

- Pen or pencil
- Diffuser with essential oils (recommended but not imperative to have)
- Music that inspires you
- Light snack and something to drink

# ESSENTIAL OILS AND THEIR IMPACT ON YOUR VISION BOARD JOURNEY

Essential oils are potent aromatic extracts that are distilled or expressed from various aromatic plant parts, such as flowers, fruits, leaves, resins, roots, seeds, and more.

They are potent physical healers, with some considered more powerful than herbs. They support our physical health, while also offering the energy necessary to connect with our emotions deeply, making them ideal to help you with the process of making your Vision Board.

Every essential oil and blend carries its unique emotional resonance, this makes them powerful instruments in the creation of your Vision Board. Furthermore, they play a crucial role in bringing your dreams and desires to life through manifestation.

# A FEW BENEFITS OF ACCOMPANYING THE PROCESS WITH ESSENTIAL OILS

They stimulate the senses

They provide focus and concentration

They help reduce stress and anxiety

They ground, connect and promote emotional balance

They encourage creativity

They motivate and energize

They promote reflection

They inspire intuition

They create a harmonious environment

# SOME ESSENTIAL OILS THAT CAN HELP YOU IN THE PROCESS

## and their emotional significance

### Melissa
### The Oil of Light

Encourages the release of anything interfering with your true potential. It aids in letting go of what does not align with your inner light.

# SOME ESSENTIAL OILS THAT CAN HELP YOU IN THE PROCESS

## and their emotional significance

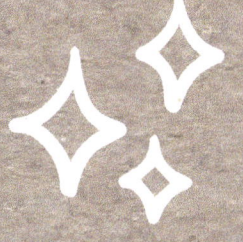

### Copaiba
### The Oil of Unveiling

Prompts us to begin the process of unraveling and restoring, crucial for long lasting healing, for enhanced awareness, and for deeper insight.

# SOME ESSENTIAL OILS THAT CAN HELP YOU IN THE PROCESS

## and their emotional significance

### Bergamot
### The Oil of Self-Acceptance

Provides support during moments requiring self-acceptance and self-love, fostering a more optimistic outlook on life and easing feelings of self-doubt.

# SOME ESSENTIAL OILS THAT CAN HELP YOU IN THE PROCESS

## and their emotional significance

### Frankincense
### The Oil of Truth

Encourages letting go of deceit, paving the way for fresh, truthful perspectives. It uncovers false beliefs, connecting the soul to reveal the truth.

# SOME ESSENTIAL OILS THAT CAN HELP YOU IN THE PROCESS

## and their emotional significance

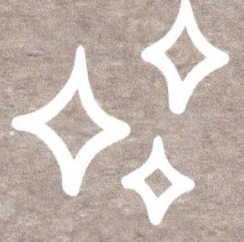

### Clary Sage
### The Oil Clarity and Vision

Unlocks the soul to embrace new possibilities and new experiences, particularly during healing phases requiring significant changes in perception.

# SOME ESSENTIAL OILS THAT CAN HELP YOU IN THE PROCESS

## and their emotional significance

### Green Mandarin
### The Oil True Potential

Serves as a reminder of our unlimited potential and endless opportunities. Its vibrant and cheerful aroma reignites our enthusiasm for life's wonders.

# WITH THIS KNOWLEDGE, LETS MAKE EITHER OF THESE BLENDS FOR DIFFUSING WHILE YOU MAKE YOUR VISION BOARD

**Add these drops to diffuser:**

3 Melissa
1 Copaiba
2 Bergamot

**Or ad these instead:**

2 Frankincense
1 Clary Sage
3 Green Mandarin

**FEEL FREE TO BLEND THEM DIFFERENTLY IF YOU WANT!**

If you don't have essential oils, don't let this stop you from making your Vision Board! They are a great tool to aide you in this process, but they are certainly not obligatory!

And if you have different oils - just not the ones mentioned before, feel free to make your own diffuser blend with them. Let your intuition guide you!

# STEP 2: SOUL REFLECTION SESSION

Before cropping the first image, you have to have **INTENTION** and **CLARITY.**

Without distractions and in a comfortable place, with love and an open heart and mind, ask yourself what you truly desire.
Let your ego step aside, and write down the answers to these questions BEFORE flipping through the images, words, phrases and abundance checks provided in this book.

# STEP 2: SOUL REFLECTION SESSION

*answer these questions*

If money, others' opinions, judgments, and my fears held no influence, what desires would I truly want to pursue, achieve, or manifest?

What beliefs must I release to invite this reality into my life? What beliefs no longer serve me?

What beliefs must I embrace to manifest or welcome this into my life?

What is truly important to me? What do I genuinely care about?

# STEP 2: SOUL REFLECTION SESSION

Reflect on your desires and take into consideration what is working in your life and what is not. **Identify the aspects of your life where you seek enhancement -** whether in career, family, relationships, health, spirituality, finances, or any other area. Create individual lists of goals for each category you want to prioritize this year or over the span of a few years.

*To bring about change in your life, you need a clear destination in mind.*

It could be helpful if after choosing the areas of your life that you would like to focus on, you list up to three goals / initiatives per area. From there, you can narrow it down to **one goal per area,** and you could even find yourself narrowing it down to fewer areas, depending on your priorities.

Use these pages to write down
your answers and your thoughts.

# STEP 3: BROWSE AND CUT

Now that you've taken notes and connected with yourself, flip through the images in this book to get an idea of the ones you want to use.

Cut out the images/words/phrases that speak to you (don't paste yet!)

They can be specific images (a house for example), or images that evoke a desired feeling in you.

# STEP 4: CHOOSE

Go through all the images, words, affirmations and checks you selected, review each one and choose the ones you want to paste on your board.

**IMPORTANT:** Be careful not to have too many images, as **saturating your mural will make you lose focus.** Choose just a few so it doesn't look chaotic or confusing.

# STEPS 5 AND 6: ARRANGE AND GLUE

If your board encompasses various aspects of life, you can assign a theme for each quadrant, for example: work, relationships, spirituality, health. In the center, you could place a photo of yourself that you really like and that represents what you desire. If you'd rather not use a photo of yourself, that's ok too!

According to **Feng Shui,** you can arrange the images according to the **'bagua' map,** which is the distribution of energy within your home. It's a tool used to identify areas of the house in relation to different aspects of life.

TOP TIPS

# 9 GRID VERSION OF BAGUA MAP

| | | |
|---|---|---|
| Golden<br>Purple<br>Blue<br><br>Wealth and Prosperity | Red<br><br>Fame, Recognition and Reputation | Pink<br>White<br><br>Love and Relationships |
| Green<br>Blue<br><br>General health and Relationships Relatives | Yellow<br>Orange<br>Coffee<br>Wellness (this area represents you, add your photo) | White<br>Silver<br>Copper<br><br>Children and Creativity |
| Blue<br>Green<br><br>Wisdom and Self-knowledge | Black<br>Dark Blue<br>Coal<br><br>Career, Work, Life Mission | Grey<br>Silver<br>Metallic<br><br>Travel<br>Helpful people |

# STEP 7: DECORATE

Once everything is glued in place, start decorating. You can use decorations like stamps, stickers, paint, glitter, etc. Just remember to **NOT SATURATE IT** so you don't lose focus.

*At this time, you can add your word of the year if you have it*

# STEP 8: GIVE THANKS

After creating your mural, **express your gratitude to the universe.** Know that you are already receiving what you dream of and are working towards, and be wholeheartedly grateful for it.

Feel that feeling that you are looking for with the achievement of your goals and dreams, and take some time to be grateful for the blessings that are on your vision board and therefore, in your life.

# STEP 9: MAKE A COPY, TAKE A PHOTO

Once finished, make a reduced copy to carry in your wallet, or take a photo and print it out for easy access.

Have the photo of your board as your phone wallpaper. You can also set it as your computer background for easy access and frequent inspiration.

*Looking at your vision board frequently helps you reflect on your goals and take the action needed to make them come true*

# STEP 10: DISPLAY YOUR BOARD

Choose an **IMPORTANT** place in your home to hang it, somewhere you'll see it when waking up and before going to bed, **at the very least.**

Every time you see it, **take a few minutes to really look** at every image, every word, every phrase and think about the actions you are taking towards achieving your goals.

Make sure you hang it in a **clutter-free area** to avoid distractions

If possible, surround your vision board with items or elements that **complement your goals,** like plants or objects that resonate with your aspirations.

# STEP 10: DISPLAY YOUR BOARD

Hang your vision board in an area that promotes **positivity and good energy flow**, avoiding spaces that feel stagnant or negative. Don't put it where the toilet is!

Adjust or change anything in your vision board if it **no longer serves you**, this includes where you place it. Recenter and refocus yourself regularly!

If your goals are **personal or sensitive**, consider placing your it in a more secluded area, where you can reflect without distraction or interruption.

Set up a nearby area for journaling about your goals and dreams. Write down the **daily action steps** you'll take to get closer to turning your goals into reality.

# STEP 11: USING YOUR BOARD AND TAKING ACTION

What actions can you take **EVERY DAY** to reach the goals you set for yourself? Schedule a dedicated time to work on your goals.

Take firm steps daily. **NO EXCUSES, YOU'VE GOT THIS!**

Break larger goals into **SMALLER, MORE MANAGEABLE** tasks for a clearer path forward. It also helps to share your goals with someone who can help keep you accountable (accountability partner.)

Each time you look at your board and you take action, **FEEL THE EXCITEMENT / JOY / PEACE** —the feelings you expect to experience once you reach your goals.

Remember, having a vision board won't do the work for you, but it will serve as **FOCUS, REMINDER AND INSPIRATION.**

# "NEW BEGINNINGS" ESSENTIAL OIL BLEND

2 Peppermint
4 Lemon*
2 Thyme
3 Lavender
5 Juniper Berry
2 Grapefruit*

Put them in a 10 mL roller bottle, and fill the rest with fractionated coconut oil.

Apply this blend on your skin (wrists, heart, spine, bottoms of feet) several times a day, and take a minute to inhale it and reflect on your goals and dreams.

**This is the beginning of beautiful things for you!**

*Avoid sunlight and UV rays for at least 12 hours after topically applying citrus oils.

# "NEW BEGINNINGS" ESSENTIAL OIL BLEND

*emotional meaning of each essential oil*

Peppermint → Buoyant heart

Lemon → Focus

Thyme → Releasing and forgiving

Lavender → Communication and Calm

Juniper Berry → Night (learn lessons and face fears)

Grapefruit → Honoring the Body

# "NEW BEGINNINGS" ESSENTIAL OIL BLEND

Think of this blend as a portal to personal transformation and renewal, accompanying you in a new year full of opportunity, growth and self-acceptance.

**Peppermint** invites you to start this new journey with a happy and optimistic heart, encouraging you to embrace life with enthusiasm.

**Lemon** offers you the mental clarity you need to focus on your future goals. It has a refreshing aroma that clears the mind, allowing you to focus on what really matters and fulfill your dreams.

**Thyme** guides you toward emotional release and helps you let go of what has been holding you back. It inspires you to forgive, let go of the burdens of the past, and open yourself to the new opportunities that come your way.

# "NEW BEGINNINGS" ESSENTIAL OIL BLEND

**Lavender** gives you the peace you need to communicate your thoughts and emotions clearly and calmly. It invites you to express yourself authentically and find inner tranquility when facing any challenge.

**Grapefruit** reminds you of the importance of honoring your body and taking care of your well-being. Its invigorating aroma connects you with gratitude for your body and inspires you to nourish it with love and attention.

**Juniper Berry** supports you if you fear unknown or dark aspects of yourself, helping you understand that what you fear can be a teacher. We experience more expansiveness when we reconcile with fears and hidden aspects of ourselves.

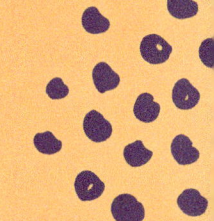

# WHAT IS AN ABUNDANCE CHECK?

An abundance check is an excellent visualization tool to reinforce your intentions and goals. You create a check made out to yourself for the amount of money you desire to fulfill those goals, and you write the check as if it's coming from an **INFINITE SOURCE OF ABUNDANCE,** not from a specific bank account.

*This check represents the abundance, wealth, or specific desires you wish to attract into your life.*

# ABUNDANCE CHECKS

When you make an abundance check, it's like a statement to yourself and the universe about what you want to manifest. **It's a tool that helps you get clear about your financial desires,** making them more tangible and real. By putting them on your vision board or keeping them in a visible place, they serve as a reminder and keep your attention on those specific financial goals.

They are effective to help you visualize your goals and stay focused on taking actions aligned with the reality you want to create.

# CLIPART WITH IMAGES, WORDS, ABUNDANCE CHECKS AND AFFIRMATIONS

Explore the collection of images and phrases in this book at your own pace. Choose the elements that truly resonate and inspire you for your Vision Board. Seek out those visuals and words that evoke the most excitement and joy within you. Remember, each selected image and phrase should ignite enthusiasm in you! It's super important to fully engage your emotions in this process. Enjoy the creation of your Vision Board!

If not now, when?

2024
HAPPY NEW YEAR

2025
HAPPY NEW YEAR

2026
HAPPY NEW YEAR

HAPPY NEW YEAR

DETOX
loading . . .

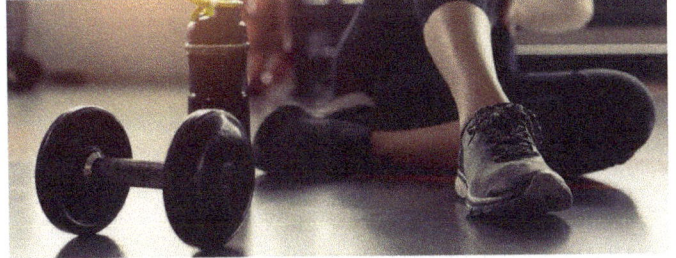

# health is wealth

SELF CARE

Discover Who You Are

# eat well feel good

 WELLNESS
 RELAXATION
 YOGA
 HEALTH
 EXERCISE
 SPA
 WELLBEING
 GRATITUDE

 BALANCED DIET
 AROMATHERAPY
 ACHIEVABLE GOALS
 SENSE OF BELONGING
 STRESS MANAGEMENT
 HERBAL MEDICINE
 OPTIMISTIC OUTLOOK
 PERSONAL GROWTH

 TAI CHI
 MEDITATION
 NUTRITION
 GOOD SLEEP
 RELATIONSHIP
 SELF-CARE
 SPIRITUALITY
 MASSAGE

love

NEVER FAILS

Forever

For Always

No matter what

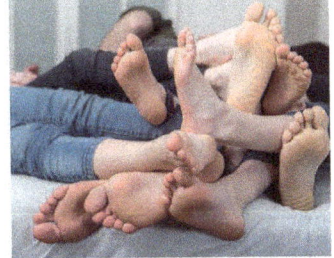

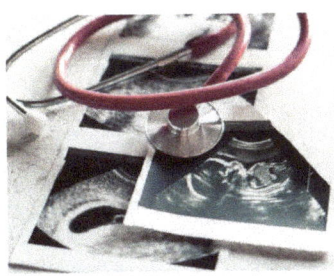

BABY
IS
COMING

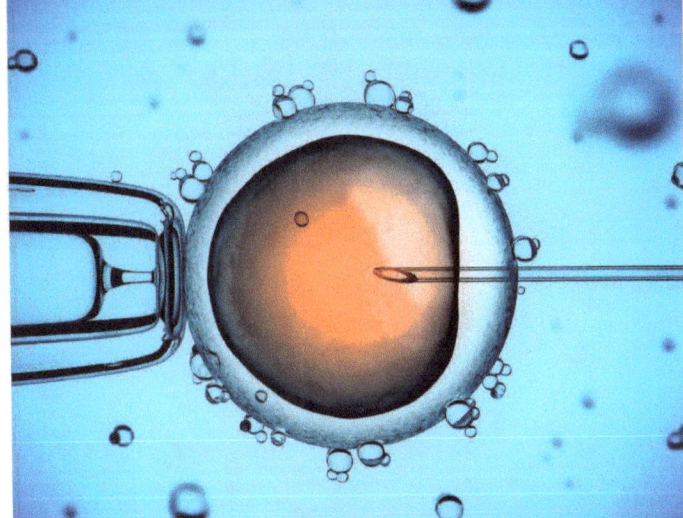

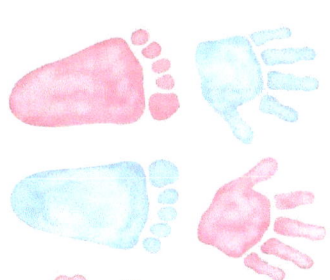
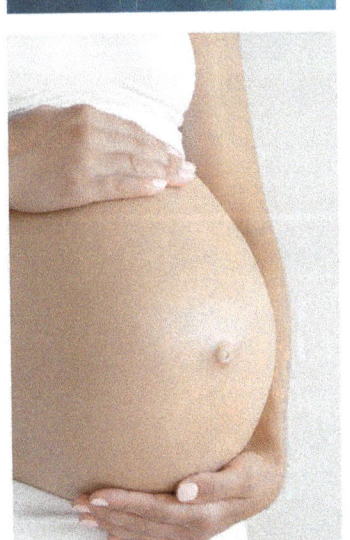

hello
little
- one -

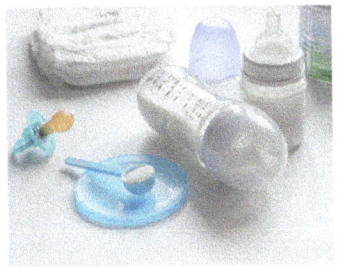

adventure
AWAITS

# WORKOUT

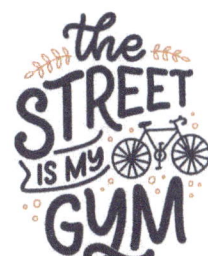

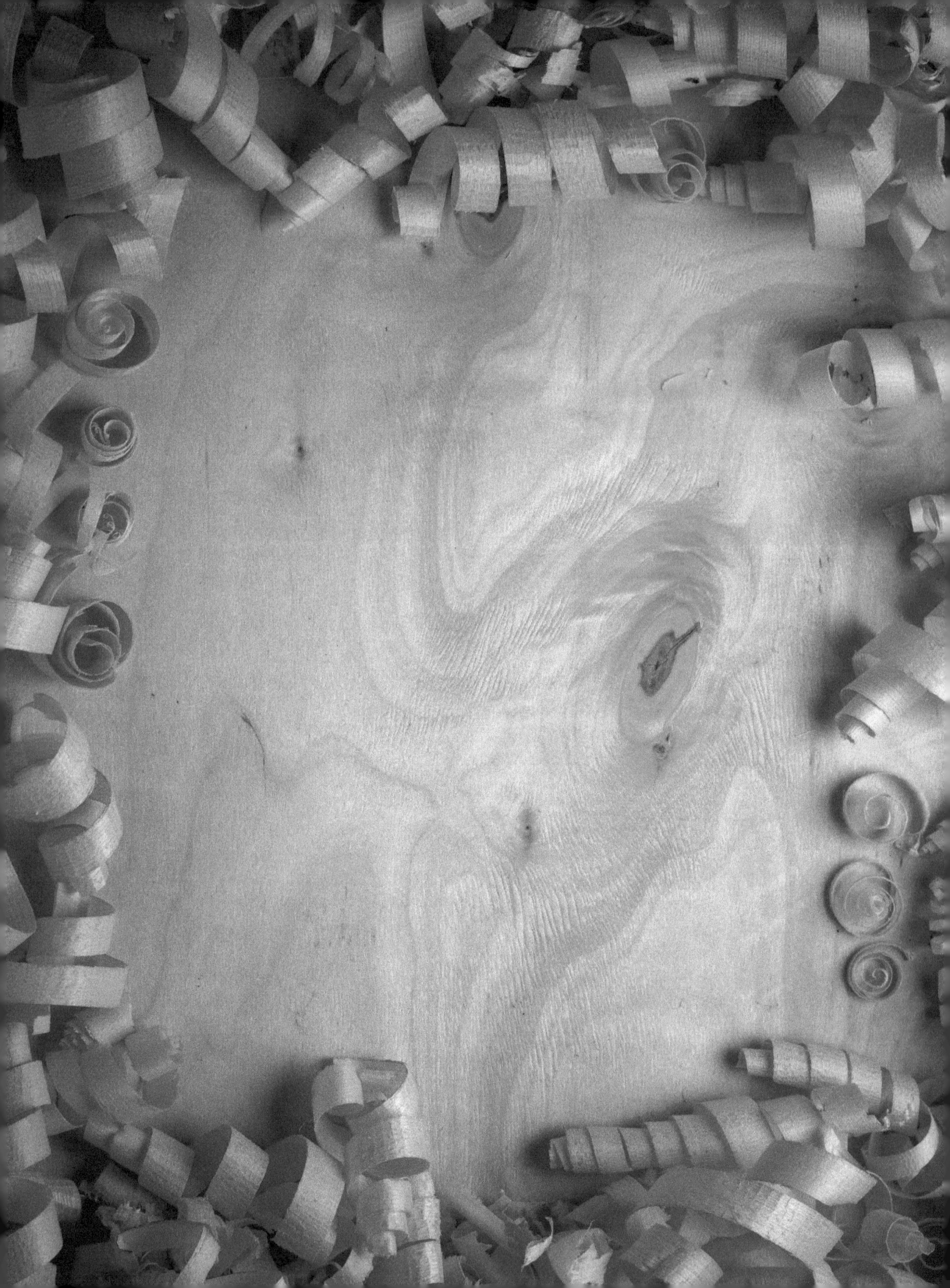

CREATIVITY

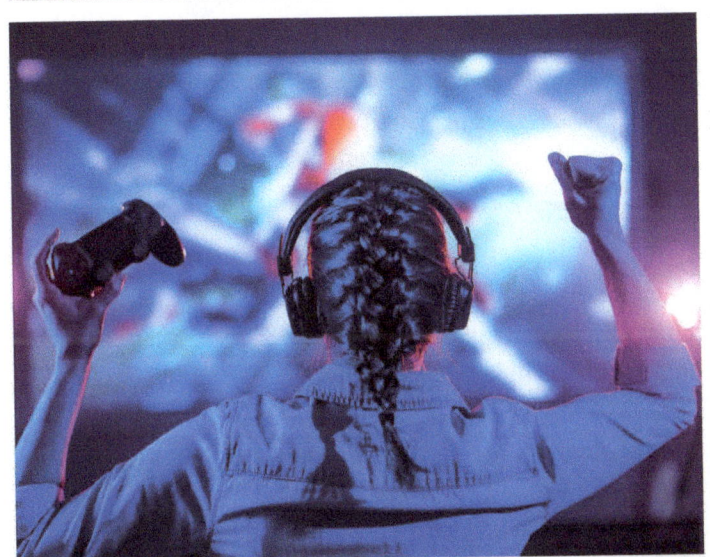

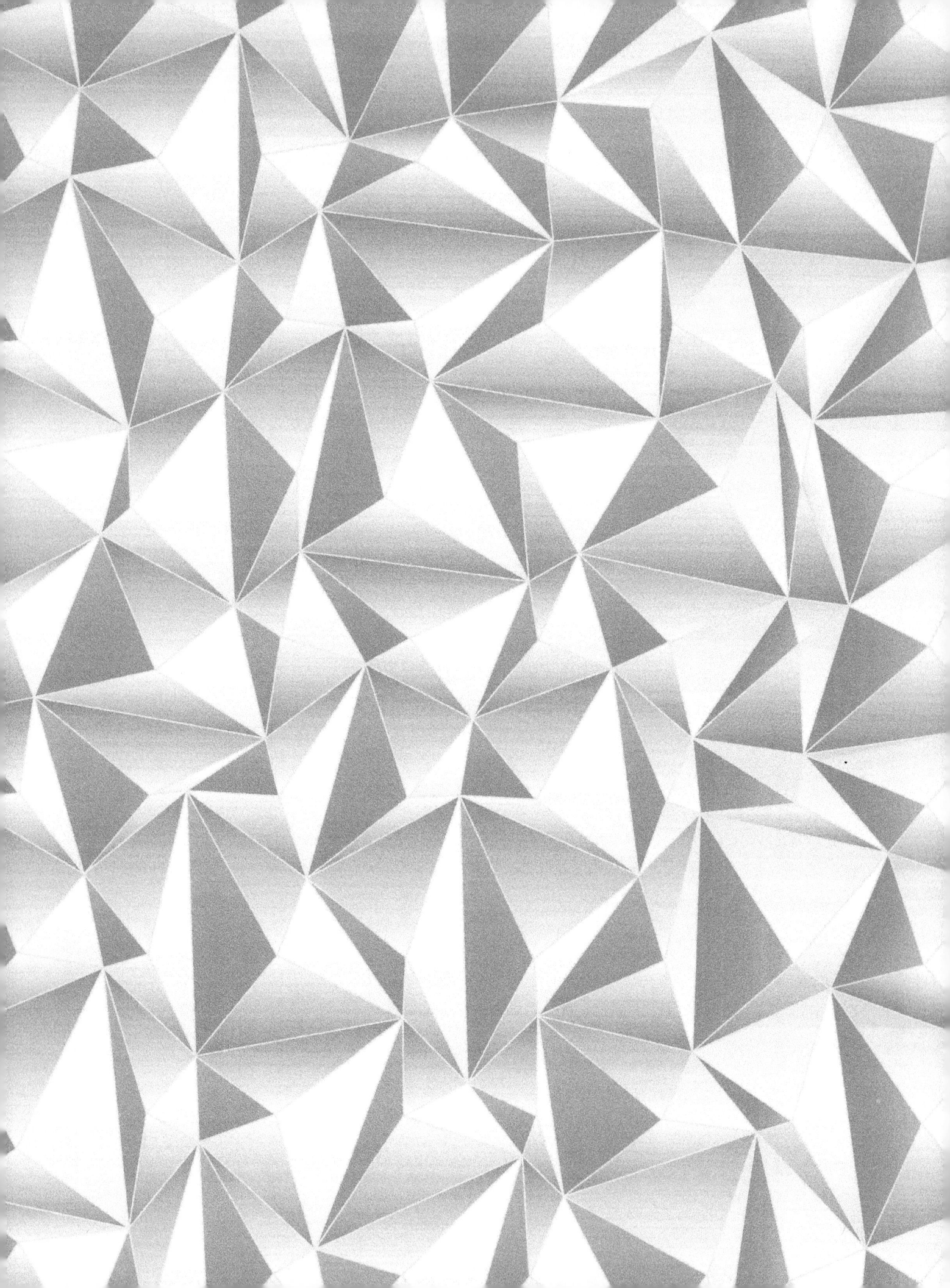

HOME
IS NOT A PLACE.
IT'S A FEELING

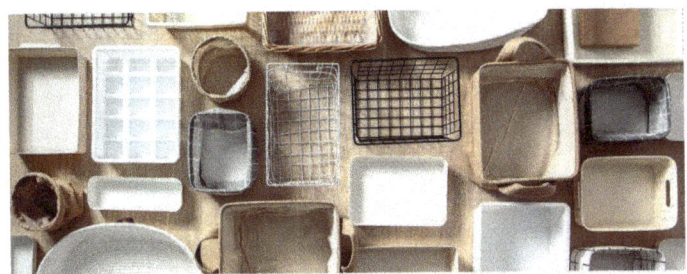

SOLD

home

WHERE YOU ARE LOVED NO MATTER WHAT

# Style

INFLUENCE

STRATEGY

CHARISMA

LEADERSHIP

TEAM BUILDING

MOTIVATION

CONFIDENCE

VISION

GUIDANCE

ORGANIZATION

GOAL

TRUST

MENTORSHIP

COLLECTIVE DIRECTION

DECISION MAKING

EMPOWERMENT

TEAMWORK

INSPIRATION

LEAD

COACHING

LEADER

REACH

CHALLENGE

COLLABORATION

THE MORE you LEARN the MORE YOU earn

## INFINITE ABUNDANCE BANK

# 111

DATE _____ _____ _____
Day   Month   Year

PAY TO THE
ORDER OF _____

$ [                    ]

_____

DOLLARS 🔒 Security
features
included.

MEMO _____

*The Universe*
Authorized signature

⑆0123456789⑆   ⑉0123789789⑉   ⑈12345⑈

## INFINITE ABUNDANCE BANK

# 888

DATE _____ _____ _____
Day   Month   Year

PAY TO THE
ORDER OF _____

$ [                    ]

_____

DOLLARS 🔒 Security
features
included.

MEMO _____

*The Universe*
Authorized signature

⑆0123456789⑆   ⑉0123789789⑉   ⑈12345⑈

## BANK NAME |
123, Lorem Str., Ipsum City
Phone 123-456-789-00

01234

DATE _____ _____ _____
Day   Mounth   Year

PAY TO THE
ORDER OF _____

$ [                    ]

_____

DOLLARS 🔒 Security
features
included.

MEMO _____

Authorized signature

⑆0123456789⑆   ⑉0123789789⑉   ⑈12345⑈

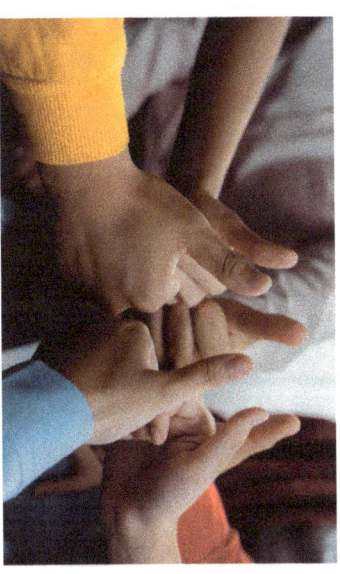

**GO where I FEEL most alive**

**~SO much WORLD so little TIME~**

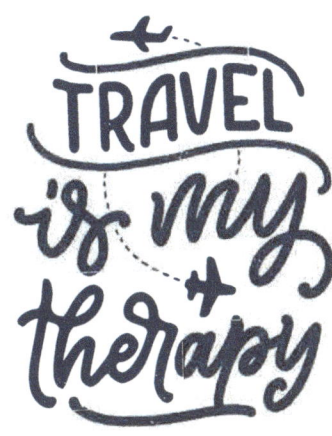
**TRAVEL is my therapy**

**Let's START the JOURNEY**

# MAKE YOUR
## —own—
# PATH

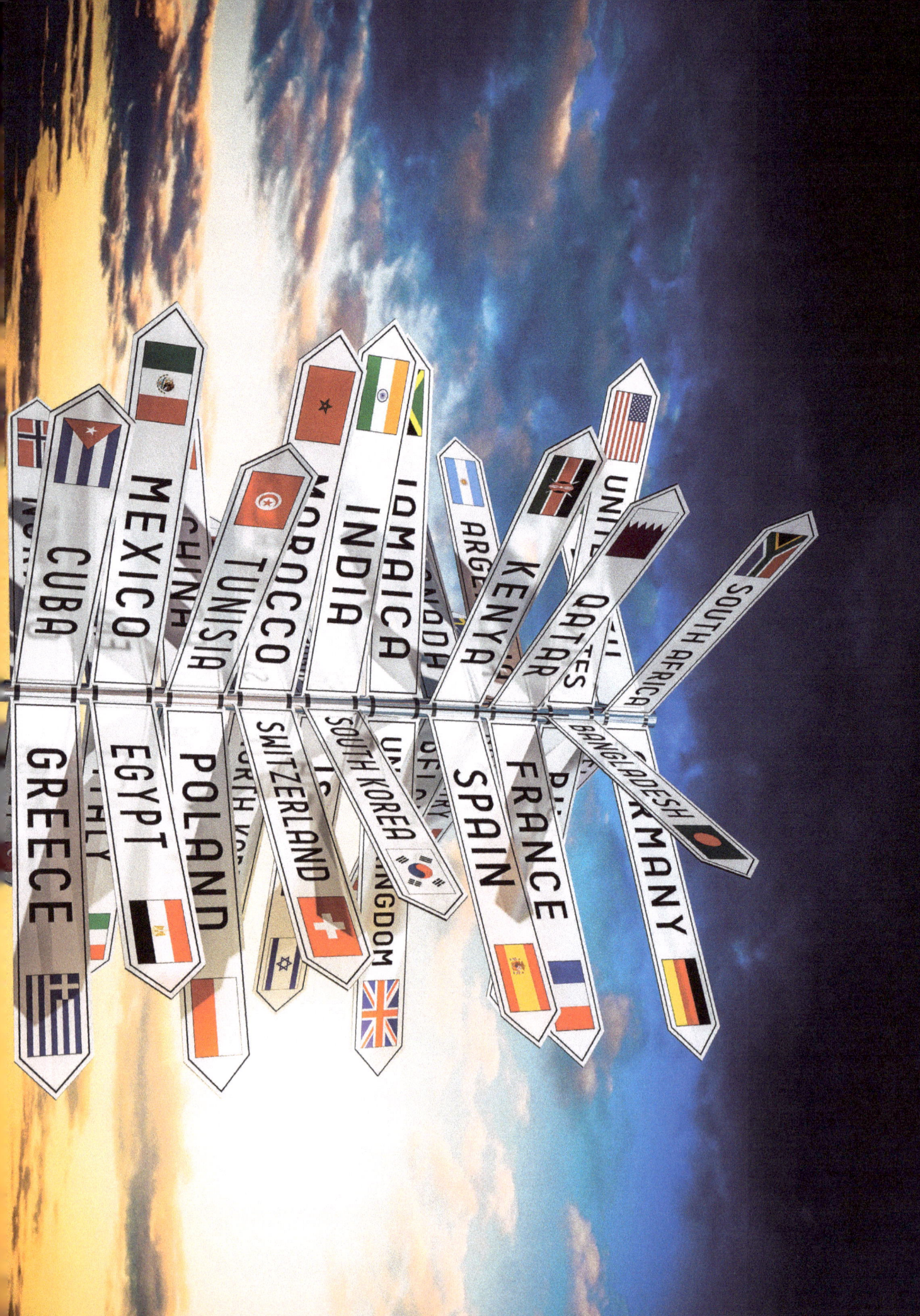

# flags of the world

| | | | | | | | |
|---|---|---|---|---|---|---|---|
| Algeria | Djibouti | Angola | | | | | Egypt |
| Barbados | India | Lebanon | Peru | Suriname | Ecuador | Guinea-Bissau | Macedonia |
| | | | | | | | Slovenia |
| Belize | Indonesia | Mauritius | Portugal | Sierra Leone | Equatorial Guinea | Honduras | Malaysia |
| | | | | | | | Solomon Islands |
| Benin | Iraq | Mozambique | Russian Federation | Thailand | Republic of South Africa | Dominica | Moldova |
| | | | | | | | Sudan |
| Burkina Faso | Spain | Mauritania | Rwanda | Tanzania | Japan | Western Sahara | Mongolia |
| | | | | | | | Tajikistan |
| Bhutan | Italy | Madagascar | Romania | Tunisia | Abkhazia | Zimbabwe | Nauru |
| | | | | | | | Tonga |
| Venezuela | Yemen | Malawi | Saudi Arabia | Turkmenistan | Australia | Jordan | Nigeria |
| | | | | | | | Tuvalu |
| Vietnam | Cameroon | Mali | Eswatini | Turkey | Azerbaijan | Ireland | New Zealand |
| | | | | | | | Uzbekistan |
| Gambia | Kenya | Maldives | Senegal | Uganda | Armenia | Kazakhstan | United Arab Emirates |
| | | | | | | | Fiji |
| Ghana | China | Malta | Saint Vincent and the Grenadines | Ukraine | Bahamas | Canada | Oman |
| | | | | | | | Philippines |
| Guinea | Colombia | Morocco | Saint Kitts and Nevis | Uruguay | Bosnia and Herzegovina | Kiribati | State of Palestine |
| | | | | | | | Croatia |
| Greece | Congo | Myanmar | Serbia | France | Belarus | North Korea | Paraguay |
| | | | | | | | Montenegro |

Northern Cyprus
Chad
Namibia
Cook Islands
Iceland

South Ossetia
Costa Rica
Kosovo
Sweden
Taiwan
Brunei
Eritrea
Cyprus
Monaco

Jamaica
Lithuania
Papua New Guinea
Togo
Singapore
Cuba
Ethiopia
Kyrgyzstan
Denmark

Bangladesh
Liechtenstein
San Marino
Finland
Donetsk People's Republic
Samoa
South Sudan
Comoros
Gabon

Bahrain
Luxembourg
Israel
Iran
Luhansk People's Republic
Sri Lanka
United Kingdom
Kuwait
Guatemala

Bulgaria
Nicaragua
Norway
Mexico
Republic of Artsakh
Cape Verde
Hungary
Latvia
Saint Lucia

Burundi
El Salvador
Andorra
Liberia
Pridnestrovian Moldavian Republic
Niger
East Timor
Libya
Seychelles

Vanuatu
Trinidad and Tobago
Afghanistan
Federated States of Micronesia
Somaliland
Estonia
Netherlands
Syria
Czech Republic

Haiti
Nepal
Brazil
United States of America
Azad Kashmir
Niue
Pakistan
Slovakia
Chile

Guyana
Vatican
Bolivia
Qatar
Marshall Islands
Austria
Albania
Somalia
Central African Republic

Germany
Switzerland
Argentina
Botswana
Georgia
South Korea
Palau
Sao Tome and Principe
Ivory Coast

Grenada
Belgium
Cambodia
Dominican Republic
Laos
Lesotho
Democratic Republic of the Congo
Poland
Antigua and Barbuda

THINK
OUTSIDE
THE
BOX

ALL YOU NEED IS
# LOVE
ALWAYS & FOREVER

# life is BETTER —WITH— Friends

# PEACE LOVE JOY & TREATS

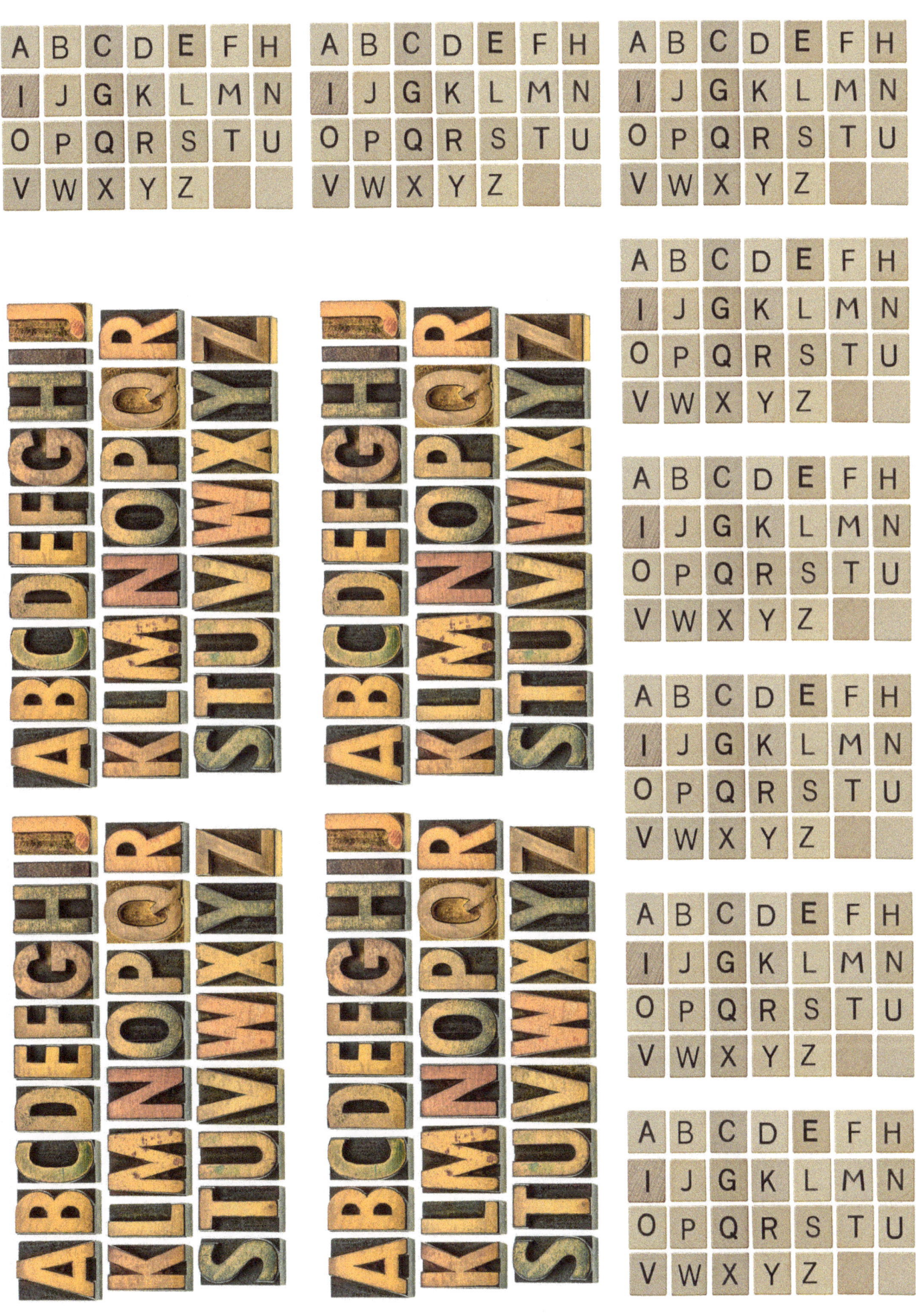

I AM THE ARCHITECT OF MY DREAMS

MY POTENTIAL IS LIMITLESS

I ATTRACT SUCCESS EFFORTLESSLY

I AM A FORCE OF POSITIVE CHANGE

MY DREAMS ARE VALID AND ACHIEVABLE

I EMBRACE THE JOURNEY TO MANIFEST MY GOALS

I TRUST IN MY ABILITY TO CREATE MY REALITY

CONFIDENCE FUELS MY MANIFESTING POWER

I AM DESERVING OF MY DREAMS COMING TRUE

I RELEASE ANY SCARCITY MINDSET AND WELCOME
THE BOUNDLESS PROSPERITY THAT SURROUNDS ME

I RADIATE STRENGTH AND RESILIENCE

**I AM A MAGNET FOR ABUNDANCE AND OPPORTUNITIES**

**MY DREAMS ALIGN WITH MY PURPOSE**

**I AM EMPOWERED TO OVERCOME ANY OBSTACLE**

**I AM THE AUTHOR OF MY SUCCESS STORY**

**I AM SURROUNDED BY SUPPORTIVE ENERGY**

**I EMBRACE THE JOURNEY TO MANIFEST MY GOALS**

**WEALTH IS A NATURAL AND JOYFUL PART OF MY LIFE**

**I AM OPEN TO NEW STREAMS OF INCOME**

**I AM ALIGNED WITH THE ENERGY OF WEALTH**

**THE UNIVERSE IS CONSPIRING FOR MY PROSPERITY**

I PRIORITIZE MY WELL-BEING AND MAKE
CHOICES THAT NURTURE MY HEALTH

MY BODY IS A TEMPLE, AND I TREAT
IT WITH LOVE AND RESPECT

I AM IN HARMONY WITH MY BODY, MIND, AND SPIRIT

EVERY BREATH I TAKE FILLS ME WITH VITALITY AND ENERGY

I AM GRATEFUL FOR MY HEALTHY AND VIBRANT LIFE

I CHOOSE NOURISHING FOODS THAT
SUPPORT MY OVERALL WELL-BEING

MY BODY IS RESILIENT, AND I TRUST ITS ABILITY TO HEAL

I AM SURROUNDED BY A HEALING ENERGY
THAT PROMOTES WELL-BEING

I AM GRATEFUL FOR THE ABUNDANT
HEALTH THAT FLOWS THROUGH ME

EVERY CELL IN MY BODY VIBRATES WITH
HEALTH AND VITALITY

I AM MINDFUL OF THE BALANCE
BETWEEN WORK, REST, AND PLAY

I AM A SPIRITUAL BEING HAVING A
FULFILLING HUMAN EXPERIENCE

MY SOUL IS CONNECTED TO THE DIVINE
SOURCE OF LOVE AND LIGHT

I TRUST THE JOURNEY OF MY SPIRITUAL GROWTH

EVERY EXPERIENCE IS A LESSON FOR MY
SOUL'S BEAUTIFUL EVOLUTION

I AM OPEN TO THE GUIDANCE OF MY INNER WISDOM

I AM ONE WITH THE UNIVERSE, AND IT
SUPPORTS ME ON MY SPIRITUAL PATH

MY SPIRITUALITY IS A SOURCE OF
STRENGTH AND RESILIENCE

I AM GRATEFUL FOR THE GUIDANCE AND BLESSINGS
THAT ACCOMPANY ME ON MY SPIRITUAL JOURNEY

I SURRENDER TO THE DIVINE PLAN,
TRUSTING IN ITS PERFECTION

I AM A VESSEL FOR DIVINE LOVE AND
A SOURCE OF POSITIVE ENERGY

# WRITE YOUR OWN AFFIRMATIONS OR EMPOWERING BELIEFS:

GIRL POWER

STEP by STEP

EVERY journey NEEDS A first STEP

Perfectly imperfect

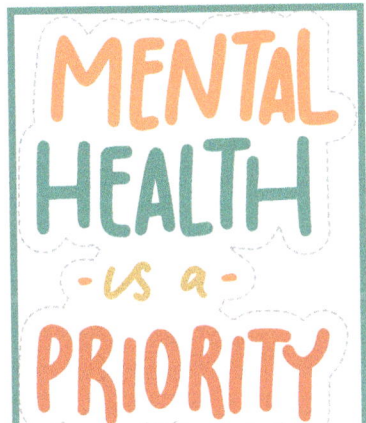
MENTAL HEALTH -is a- PRIORITY

STRONGER Than Yesterday

WELLNESS

keep GOING

DON'T QUIT

Mental health matters

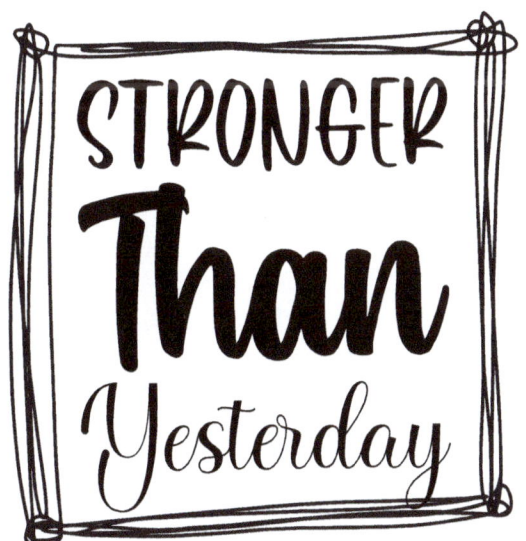
take care of your mind

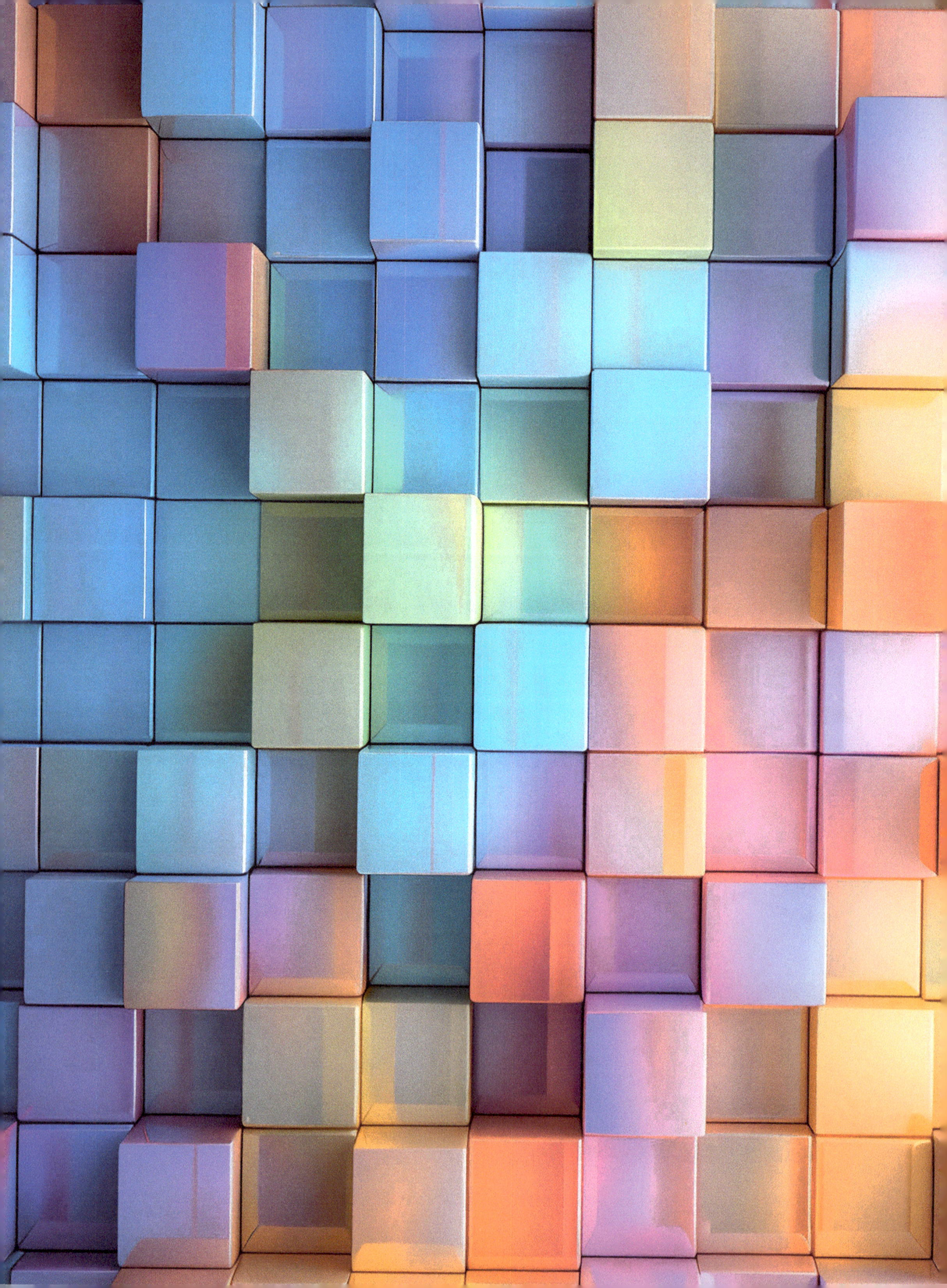

Quiet
THE
MIND

HUSTLE
for the
MUSCLE

MENTAL
health
MATTERS

STRONG
LIKE A
MOTHER

· I AM ·
STRONG

YOGA IS...
magic

IT
always
SEEMS
IMPOSSIBLE
until IT'S
DONE

· make ·
YOURSELF
a
PRIORITY

BE
STRONG

PROGRESS
- NOT -
Perfection

I AM A
SURVIVOR

Health
is wealth

make **Yourself** Proud.

One day AT A TIME

EAT *well* FEEL *good*

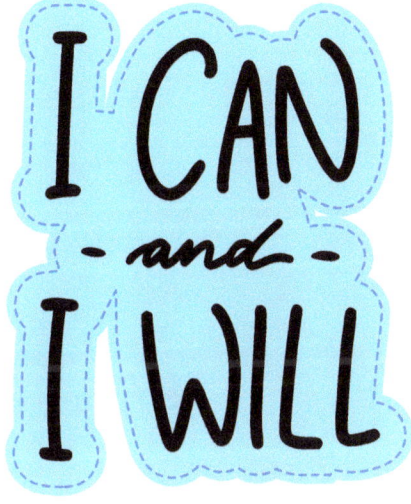

I CAN - and - I WILL

*Be* Your Best

Be HEALTHY eat HEALTHY

NO *body* IS *Perfect*

it's NEVER too late

Just Keep *Swimming*

GYM

WAKE UP AND *workout*

NO EXCUSES #

Every Journey NEEDS A First Step

Positive mind

You're doing great!

Just A Girl With Goals

Step out of your comfort ZONE.

Take care of YOURSELF

Fitness

IT'S SIMPLE, JUST GO RUN

DON'T FORGET TO TAKE A BREAK

Make it happen Shock everyone

Dear Body, I love you

Body positive

love your body

all bodies are good bodies

TAKE CARE OF YOUR MIND

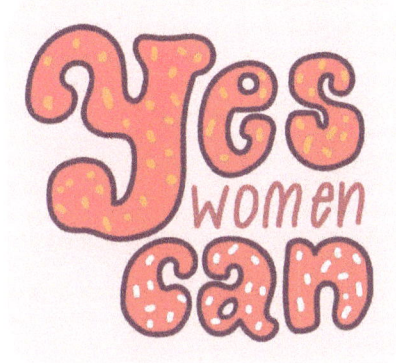

Yes women can

START NOW

DRINK MORE WATER

"be the BEST version of you"

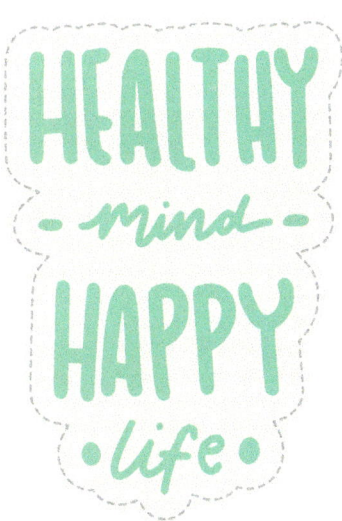

HEALTHY -mind- HAPPY life

eat sleep yoga repeat

you are MORE THAN your ILLNESS

MENTAL HEALTH

strong and healthy

I AM strong

you LOOK good

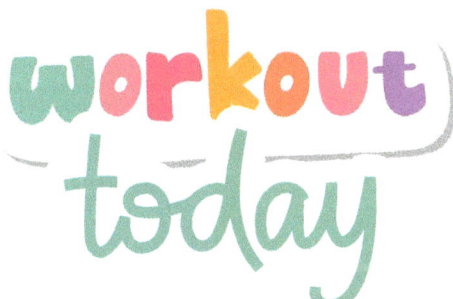
workout today

LOVE MY BODY
LOVE MY MIND

i can DO THIS

RUN FREE

fitness and health

Get moving!

LESS STRESS!

INSPIRED TO WORKOUT

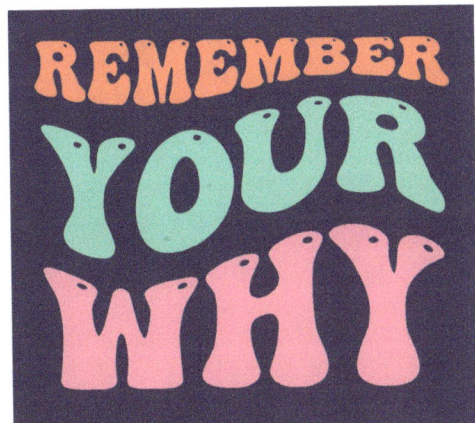

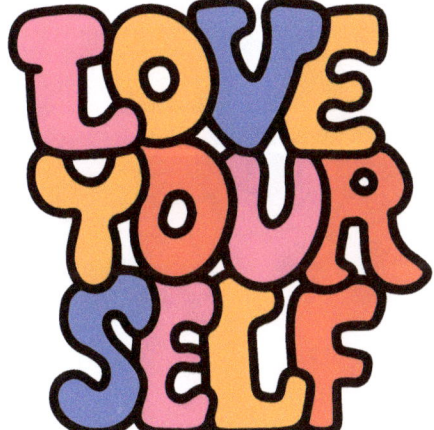

TRUST THE TIMING OF YOUR LIFE

THANKFUL grateful BLESSED

enjoy

LIVE YOUR PURPOSE

YOU DESERVE ❀ ALL JOY ❀ AND HAPPINESS

Let your light Shine

CHOOSE kindness

BELIEVE BELIEVE BELIEVE

DO YOUR BEST

Magic happens every day

Why FIT IN when you were born to STAND OUT?

WALK at your own PACE

I CAN - and - I WILL

beautiful

You Can Do ANYTHING

WAKE UP & SLAY

be happy

Believe

DON'T STOP UNTIL YOU'RE PROUD

Stay Wild

choose happy

everything will be OK

GOAL Digger

TAKE the RISK

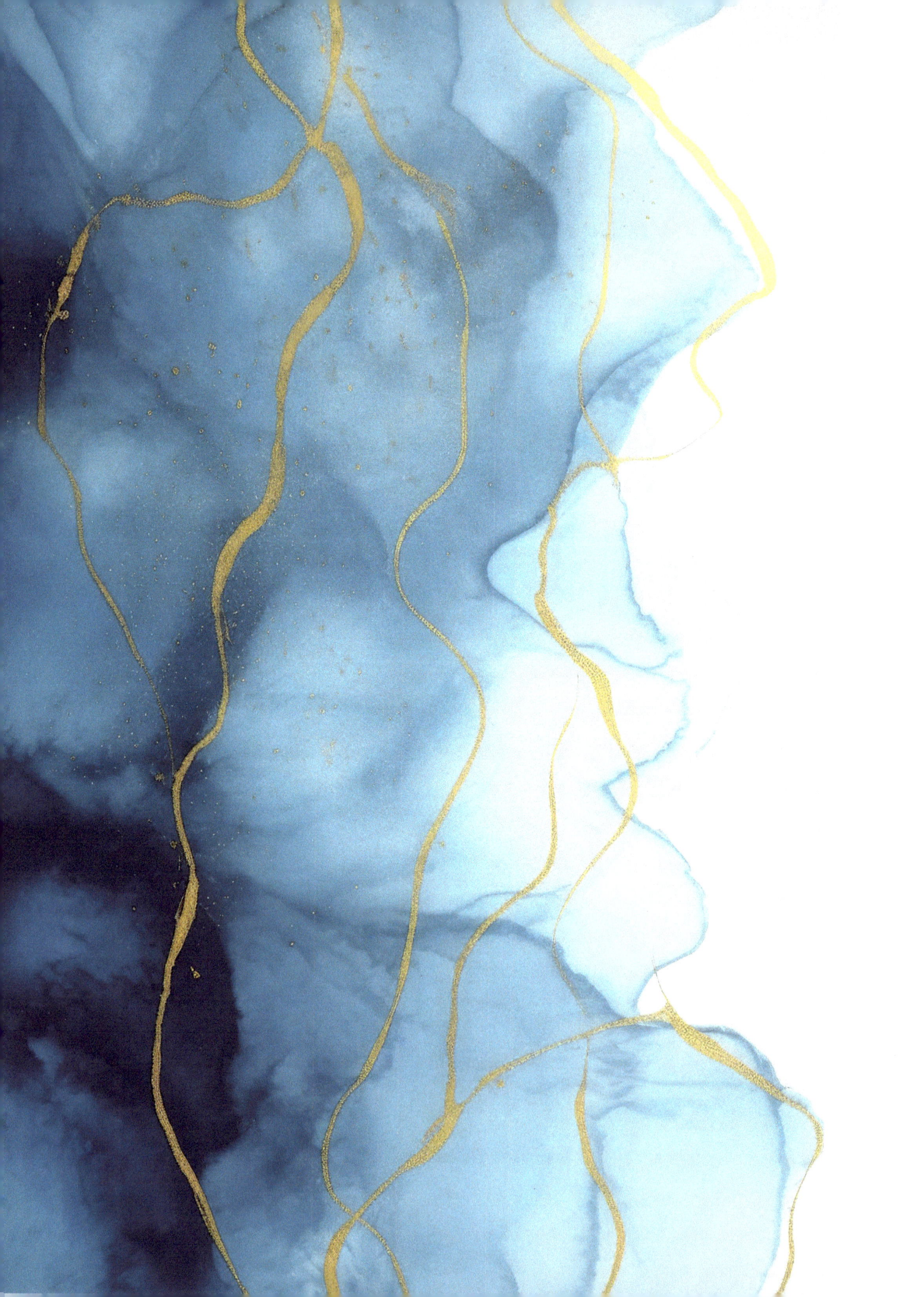

my voice matters

I will succeed

i am WORTHY

i am grateful

I am STRONG

i am GROWING

i am capable

I am loved

i am ENOUGH

I am RADIANT

I BELIEVE *in* my self

my best *is* enough

i am CONFIDENT

my voice matters

IT'S okay TO CRY

i add VALUE

I am STRONGER *than* YESTERDAY

· NO · DRAMA please

One day at a Time

WORRY LESS

this is your year

THRIVE

progress

RISE ABOVE

NEVER give UP

seek magic every day

GET IT GIRL

LOVE YOUR SELF

dream, believe, achieve

FIND YOUR fire

I DO IT FOR ME

talent HAS NO GENDER

I SLAY, OKAY

Make your own Luck

PROTECT YOUR PEACE

FOCUS ON THE GOOD

DREAM BIG AND CREATE YOUR OWN STORY

dream plan do

Make It HAPPEN

TRY AGAIN all is well dream big

you are not alone

SUCCESSFUL WOMAN

WHEN THINGS CHANGE INSIDE YOU. things CHANGE AROUND YOU

Don't let insecure thoughts ruin something amazing.

THINK IT, WANT IT, GET IT

IF YOU NEVER TRY YOU NEVER KNOW

I am loved

I am a QUEEN

I CAN DO ANYTHING I SET MY MIND TO

"I am" SUCCESSFUL

Make
TODAY
Epic

MOVE FORWARD
Good
Things
ARE
UP AHEAD

TRUST YOURSELF
You Can
do THIS

YOU'RE
Free
to BE
DIFFERENT

DON'T
JUST
FLY
SOAR!

KEEP
hustling
TO THE
FINISH LINE

YOU HAVE THE POWER to Protect YOUR PEACE

BE Gentle WITH YOURSELF

Make Yourself SEEN & HEARD

DO MORE OF WHAT YOU Love

YOU HAVE THE COURAGE TO BEGIN AGAIN

Allow Yourself Joy

trust your JOURNEY

time to TRAVEL

Let's CRUISE

Happy Camper Happy

See THE World

Let the Sea set you Free

PASSPORT

ADVENTURE

ENJOY every Sunset

The Mountains ARE Calling and I MUST GO

HAPPINESS Come in WAVES

ENJOY THE TRIP

Collect ADVENTURES Not Things

Live TO Wander

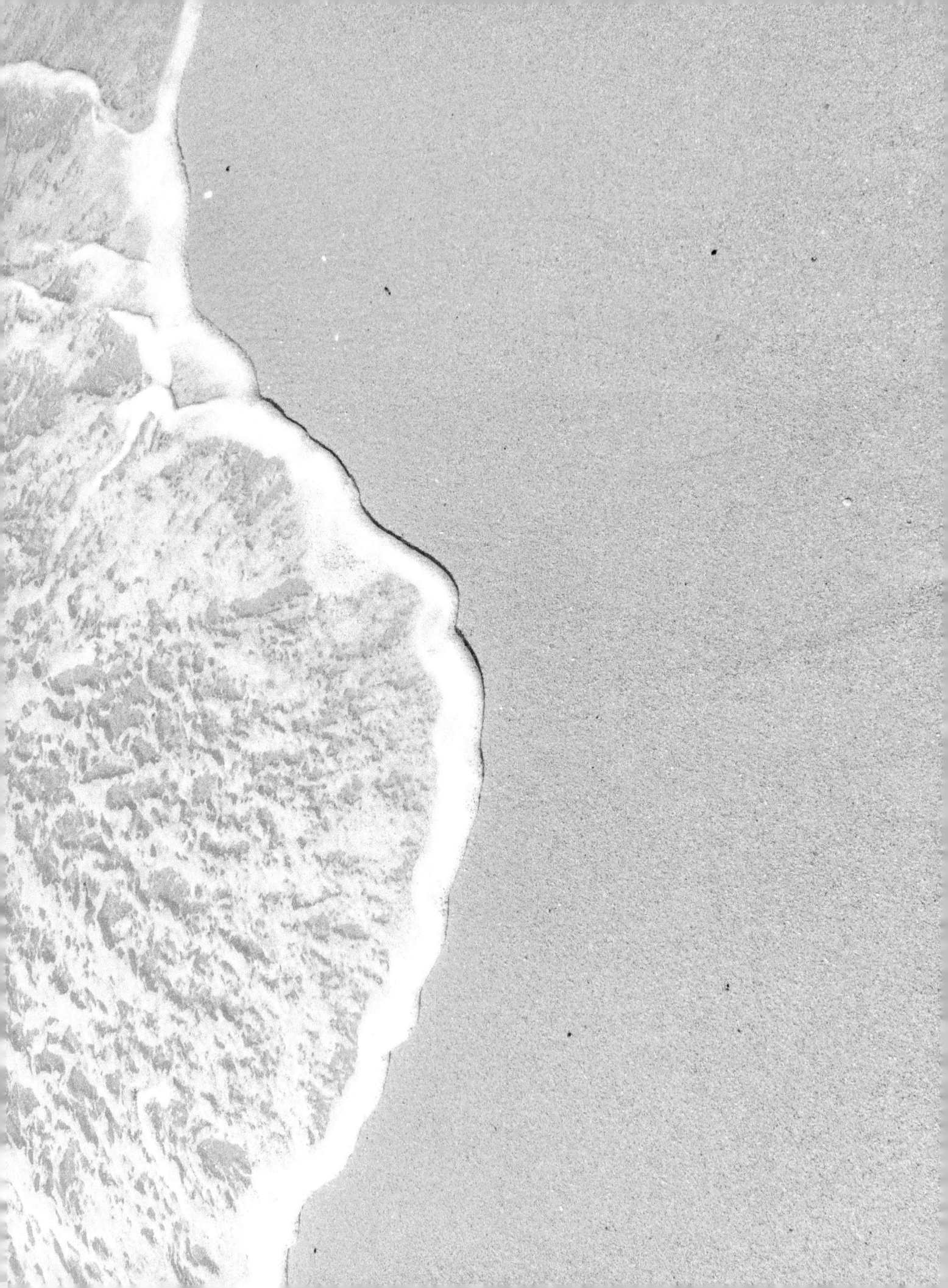

Travel BUDDIES

adventure is CALLING

EXPLORE EXPLORE

Live To Wander

Bon Voyage

Resting Beach FACE

Capture Memories

TRAVEL

I LIKE TO Be Outdoors AS MUCH AS Possible

TRAVEL THE WORLD

LET'S SLEEP UNDER The START

GOD IS WITHIN ME, GUIDING MY EVERY STEP

I AM A DIVINE CREATION, A
REFLECTION OF GOD'S LOVE.

I TRUST IN GOD'S TIMING FOR ALL
ASPECTS OF MY LIFE

MASTER MONEY MANIFESTOR

manifest it

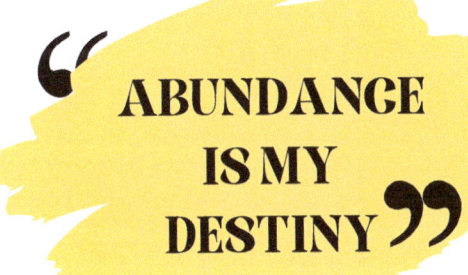

"ABUNDANCE IS MY DESTINY"

MONEY Makes MY HEART go PITTER PATTER

Money Is Calling

I am a magnet for wealth

Money Makes The World GO ROUND

STAY Humble Hustle HARD

I AM WEALTHY

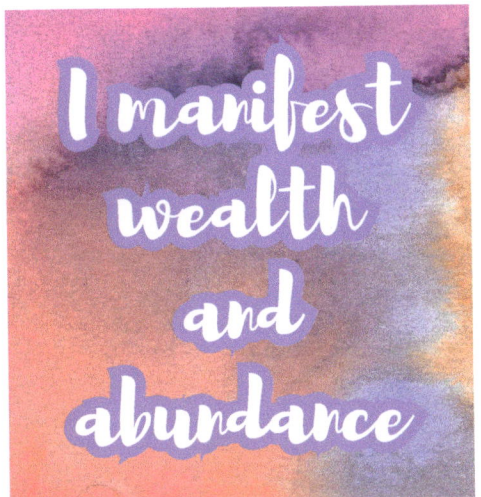

**MY FIRST**
*million*

I MAKE MILLIONS

MILLIONS MANIFESTED

THE UNITED STATES OF AMERICA

YOU CAN MAKE A MILLION EXCUSES, OR YOU CAN MAKE A MILLION DOLLARS

WEALTH UNLEASHED

MILLIONS MULTIPLY

FINE GOLD 999.9

NET WT 1000 g

THIS IS THE YEAR I BECOME RICH

THE UNIVERSE IS ABUNDAND AND I TAP INTO ITS WEALTH

# INSTRUCTIONS TO DOWNLOAD YOUR FREE BONUS

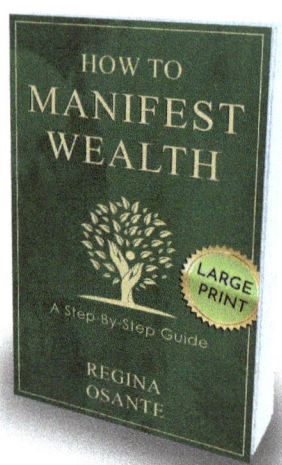

Write a (review) and download your (bonus)

## Go online to:

### FREDDOPUB.COM/ABUNDANCE

or scan the QR code with your phone camera

# Vision Board Clip Art Book
## Step-by-step Guide & Workbook

**Paperback     ISBN: 978-1-961164-07-9**

Freddo Publishing

Published by Freddo Publishing
Printed in the United States of America
Freddopub.com
Clearwater, FL 33761
United States